TECHNOLOGY OF THE ANCIENTS

THE MESOPOTAMIANS

WIL MARA

mc Marshall Cavendish
Benchmark
New York

This publication represents the opinions and views of the author based on the author's personal experience, knowledge, and research. The information in this book serves as a general guide only. The author and publisher have used their best efforts in preparing this book and disclaim liability rising directly and indirectly from the use and application of this book.

Other Marshall Cavendish Offices:

Marshall Cavendish International (Asia) Private Limited, 1 New Industrial Road, Singapore 536196 ● Marshall Cavendish International (Thailand) Co Ltd. 253 Asoke, 12th Flr, Sukhumvit 21 Road, Klongtoey Nua, Wattana, Bangkok 10110, Thailand ● Marshall Cavendish (Malaysia) Sdn Bhd, Times Subang, Lot 46, Subang Hi-Tech Industrial Park, Batu Tiga, 40000 Shah Alam, Selangor Darul Ehsan, Malaysia

Marshall Cavendish is a trademark of Times Publishing Limited

All websites were available and accurate when this book was sent to press.

Library of Congress Cataloging-in-Publication Data
Mara, Wil.
The Mesopotamians / Wil Mara.
p. cm. — (Technology of the ancients)
Includes bibliographical references and index.
Summary: "Focuses on the discoveries and inventions of the ancient Mesopotamian civilization in the areas of transportation, agriculture, architecture, science, and technology"—Provided by publisher.
ISBN 978-1-60870-767-6 (print) — ISBN 978-1-60870-755-3 (ebook)
1. Iraq—Civilization—To 634—Juvenile literature.
2. Technology—Iraq—History—To 634—Juvenile literature.
3. Science—Iraq—History—To 634—Juvenile literature. I. Title. II. Series.
DS70.62.M367 2011
935--dc22

2010045266

Senior Editor: Deborah Grahame-Smith
Publisher: Michelle Bisson
Art Director: Anahid Hamparian
Series Designer: Kay Petronio

Photo research by Tracey Engel

Cover photo: Erich Lessing/Art Resource, NY

Title page: North Wind Picture Archives/AP Images

The photographs in this book are used by permission and through the courtesy of: akg-images: 7. AP Photo: Hadi Mizban, 8; North Wind Picture Archives, 30. North Wind Picture Archives: 20. Dorling Kindersley: Eric Thomas, 12 (top); Courtesy of The Science Museum, London/Dave King, 12 (bottom). The Granger Collection, New York: 13, 14, 16, 27, 36, 39, 41, 43, 45. Photo Researchers, Inc.: Sheila Terry, 17. Getty Images: SSPL, 18; Dorling Kindersley, 26; Nico Tondini, 33. The Image Works: Werner Forman/Topham, 23; SSPL, 32. Alamy: North Wind Picture Archives, 10, 24. Art Resource, NY: Erich Lessing, 34. Corbis: Herbert M. Herget/National Geographic Society, 47. SuperStock: Science and Society, 51. Danita Delimont.com: Ancient Art & Architecture, 53.

Printed in Malaysia (T)

135642

CONTENTS

CHAPTER ONE

THE LAND BETWEEN THE RIVERS

By the end of the last ice age, around 12,500 years ago, a human being's daily focus was simply to survive. Finding enough food and shelter in harsh conditions was challenging enough; building great societies was likely far from people's minds. In time, however, they began to gather in small communities, within regions rich in animal life—ideal for hunting—as well as fruits and vegetables. Reliable sources of freshwater were also essential for both drinking and farming. Soon villagers began to develop organizational structures, such as social hierarchies and labor systems. These were the first attempts at creating formalized societies that are so familiar to us now. And the people who made the greatest strides in this respect lived in the area known as Mesopotamia.

The geographic region of Mesopotamia was fairly large. Generally speaking, the bulk of it lay between the Tigris and Euphrates rivers. Today the area is represented by the nation of Iraq, along with parts of

The name Mesopotamia *comes from a Greek word meaning "between the rivers." It is believed the first settlers arrived in this region around 8000 BCE.*

eastern Syria and southeastern Turkey. The word *Mesopotamia* comes from the Greek word for "between the rivers." Researchers believe the earliest residents in the region settled along the base of the Zagros Mountains around 8000 BCE (although there is some evidence pointing to hunter-gatherer settlements that may go back as far as 11,000 BCE). The northern areas of the region had a cool, moderate climate and were suitable for satisfying basic needs, but the southern parts offered the greatest opportunities. Both the Tigris and Euphrates rivers flowed to the south, which meant the land in the southern sector was more fertile. People began developing this area relatively quickly. They started close to the waterways and gradually moved outward.

Over the next several millennia, people organized societies with simple infrastructures and government bodies. The earliest settlers were the Sumerians, located in the southern zone, who built and ran some of the first legitimate cities in human history. Other Mesopotamian groups included the Assyrians, the Babylonians, and the Amorites. These societies ruled themselves at times, ruled each other at other times, and interacted widely until they fell under the control of the Persian Empire in 539 BCE. During their multi-millennial "reign," these people conceived and executed ideas that are still used to this day. This is why Mesopotamia is often called the Cradle of Civilization.

We still have much to learn about daily life in Mesopotamia. Much of what we do know has arisen from the archaeological record—what scientists have been able to dig out of the ground or uncover elsewhere. Archaeologists must draw conclusions from relatively scant evidence that ranges from broken clay tablets to images carved into pottery or painted on crumbling walls. It is almost impossible to pin down exact dates, and it is even difficult to determine the correct century when an

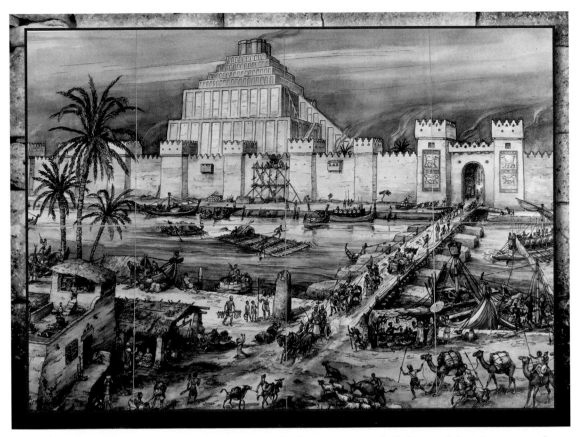

Experts believe the people of Mesopotamia were the first to structure daily human life in an organized, "civilized" way.

event occurred. Every now and then, someone will stumble across an ancient record written by someone considerate enough to include a date or a year.

Destruction and theft of artifacts has also severely limited our knowledge about Mesopotamia. For example, the recent military conflicts in Iraq have either obliterated relics by the thousands or left them vulnerable to looters, who sell the artifacts as antiques on the black market. The crucial information that these items provide usually becomes lost forever. It is as if we are trying to use just a few pieces of a jigsaw puzzle to determine its entire picture.

Many unanswered questions remain about Mesopotamia due simply to the lack of archaeological evidence. Much has been stolen through the centuries or decimated by warfare.

Nevertheless, we know enough about this magnificent bygone civilization to conclude that the Mesopotamians were the first people to make a serious attempt at organizing and structuring human life. They made huge contributions to medicine, mathematics, agriculture, and architecture. And when you consider the fact that they had few historical precedents upon which to build, their accomplishments become all the more remarkable. By the end of this book, you will no doubt see the parallels between their world—built thousands of years ago—and the one you know today.

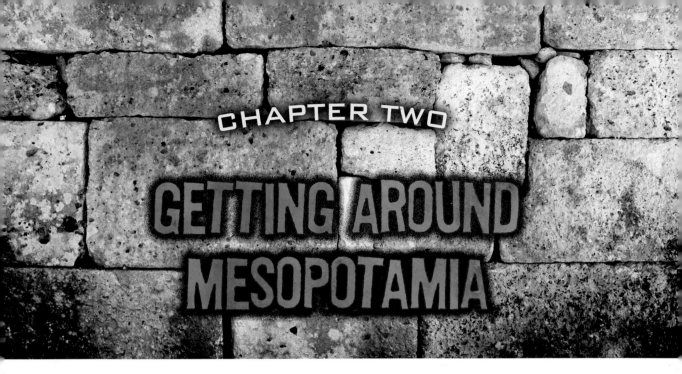

CHAPTER TWO
GETTING AROUND MESOPOTAMIA

One of humankind's greatest inventions is the wheel. When you stop to consider it, the wheel really is so simple—a disk made of anything from wood to stone to rubber, able to roll forward or backward over just about any surface. It's amazing that there was a time when wheels didn't exist.

Most experts think that the Mesopotamians—specifically the Sumerians—were responsible for the wheel's creation. This probably occurred either in the late sixth or early fifth millennium BCE. It is interesting to note that Mesopotamians might have used the first wheels in craft making, as potter's wheels, instead of as tools of transportation. This practice is still in use today. First, the potter puts a circular piece of clay onto the wheel to act as a base. Then the potter rolls more clay into long strips. As the wheel spins, the potter sets the strips onto the base one after another to build up the sides of the item. Before the creation of

The wheel was likely created in Mesopotamia some time around 6000 BCE. This illustration depicts an Assyrian monarch returning from battle in a wheeled carriage.

the wheel, potters had to apply the strips either by constantly moving the base by hand, or by getting up and moving around the table. Exhausting!

It wasn't long before someone realized that the wheel could be used for more than just making pottery. For example, it seemed like a good idea to create a vehicle for transporting people or cargo. The first archaeological evidence of a wheel being used in this way is a drawing on a Sumerian clay tablet from around 3500 BCE. The image shows four wheels supporting a sledlike platform. Soon the Sumerians were building carts, wagons, and other forms of transportation with their new invention.

The first use of the wheel was for making crafts such as pottery.

Early Mesopotamian vehicle wheels were made of wood. They did not have spokes like the wheels of a wagon from the American Old West (spokes wouldn't come into the picture until the Egyptians began using them around 2000 BCE). Instead, they were solid—sort of. The first wheels were constructed from three narrow planks laid side by side, cut into the shape of a circle, and held together by struts. You might wonder why the Mesopotamians didn't simply use one large piece of wood. Many experts believe it's

The earliest Mesopotamian wheels were made of wood—three planks cut into a circle and then held together with struts.

because they couldn't find any—there weren't trees wide enough to provide a big enough plank. The fact that the three-plank method of making wheels required cutting also supports the idea that the Mesopotamians invented the wheel because we know they used saws.

The first wheeled vehicles were most likely pushed or pulled (or both) by people. While some royalty or high government officials used vehicles powered by slaves or other servants, ordinary individuals more commonly used them to transport food and other goods. It wasn't until sometime in the third millennium BCE that people used long poles to connect animals to carts and wagons. Animals commonly used for this purpose included oxen and onagers (which are related to horses). Since the Mesopotamians lived close to the Tigris and Euphrates rivers,

Mesopotamians did not use animals to pull their earliest wheeled vehicles until some time in the third millennium BCE. Prior to that, people pushed or pulled carts and carriages themselves.

they conducted much of their transportation on water rather than on land. They did not pave roads or prepare them for vehicle travel in any other way. As a result, roads were often uneven. During rare instances of flooding, roads would turn into impassable mud pits. So, in spite of their splendid invention, the people of ancient Mesopotamia did not spend a lot of time using wheels to travel on land.

In the many thousands of years since the Mesopotamians developed their circular wonder, people have used wheels in countless ways. For

TO HAVE AND HAVE NOT

Even though the Mesopotamians appear to be the first to invent and utilize the wheel, other cultures came up with the idea, too. The wheel was developed in Europe around 2500 BCE, for example, without any known influence from the Mesopotamians. In fact, it is a bit surprising that there are ancient cultures that apparently never created a wheel. Three well-known civilizations that fall into this category are the Aztecs, the Incas, and the Mayans. Even though these societies made great strides in other technical areas, they failed to realize the wheel's tremendous potential (although there is some evidence to suggest these cultures did use wheels on toys). The same is true of the early people of North America—until the European settlers arrived, they had no wheeled vehicles or wheel-based manufacturing devices.

example, the process of milling—grinding larger items into very small particles—would have been impossible without wheels. Early construction and architecture are also indebted to the wheel—it was much easier to move heavy building materials from place to place on wheeled vehicles. Once people trained animals to pull their vehicles, people could travel longer distances than ever before. Today, wheels are so common that we barely notice them. From CDs and DVDs to the gears in a clock, the wheel is an essential component of our lives.

BOATS

The Mesopotamians were far from the first people to make use of boats. Some evidence suggests that humans were building vessels for the purpose of water travel as far back as 50,000 years ago. Some experts estimate that number is much larger—perhaps even reaching back to 130,000 BCE. The earliest boats found through archaeological excavation are about 9,000 years old. Like the great majority of boats built before them, they were made from reeds or crude wooden planks. People mostly used them locally, to travel down stream and rivers. It wasn't until later that people began building larger and sturdier boats to cross the seas and oceans.

The earliest known evidence of boat usage by the Mesopotamians comes from small models found during excavations. One description says these boats were "deep-keeled vessels with a pointed, upturned prow and stern." Another model, found in a grave from around 4000 BCE, has a shallow, bowl-like body and a mast sticking up near the middle. Around the boat's rim are a few small holes, probably for ropes that would have been tied to the mast in order to support wind sails. There was also a short pole connected horizontally inside the boat to act as a makeshift seat for the sailor. Today a simple boat like this is called a quffa or a coracle.

The Mesopotamians made extensive use of their waterways. Simple boats such as the one shown here transported people, food items, and common materials such as oil, cotton, and leather.

The Mesopotamians were sailors by nature. They had to be, for the Tigris and Euphrates rivers were, in many ways, the centerpieces of their lives. They depended on both rivers not only for water, but also as a means of travel and trade. Records show that people used boats to carry everything from vegetables, fruit, grain, and fish to basic materials such as stones, bricks, oil, cotton, and leather. The Mesopotamians also had a type of map to help them reach important places—they used written accounts of landmarks along the course of a journey rather than the illustrated maps we know today. Archaeologists have found several of these early maps on clay tablets.

Mesopotamian boats had to be built relatively small, since parts of the Tigris and Euphrates could be narrow and shallow. It was relatively easy to sail to the south along with the current. Even so, travelers often used oars or long poles for propulsion, and they used small rudders to help steer. Since the wind currents followed the same direction as the water currents, traveling back upstream could be difficult. Sails were

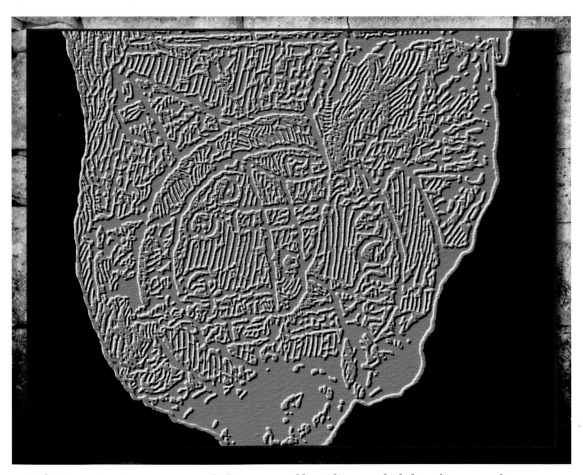

Early Mesopotamian maps were etched into stone tablets. This one, which dates from around 600 BCE, shows the ancient city of Babylon as a rectangular shape in the center, surrounded by a circle that represents a waterway.

A kelek was a large boat used to transport people and valuables not just in greater volume but also on more active rivers and even in the open seas.

useless in this situation. In shallow water, men might have to get out and push or pull the vessel along. Sometimes animals were used for the same purpose. Either way, it was a much slower journey upstream than down.

By the third millennium BCE, the Mesopotamians were building larger boats for use on broad rivers or on the open seas. There are records of Mesopotamian sailors traveling long distances in the modern-day Red Sea, the Indian Ocean, and the Persian Gulf. These improved boats are known as keleks. They were made from either wood or strong reeds, plus a type of caulking to seal the construction and to make it watertight. People made keleks more buoyant by tying inflated animal skins to the bottom and sides of the craft. Sometimes sailors would dismantle a kelek and sell its parts after reaching their destination. Then the sailors would travel back home on foot.

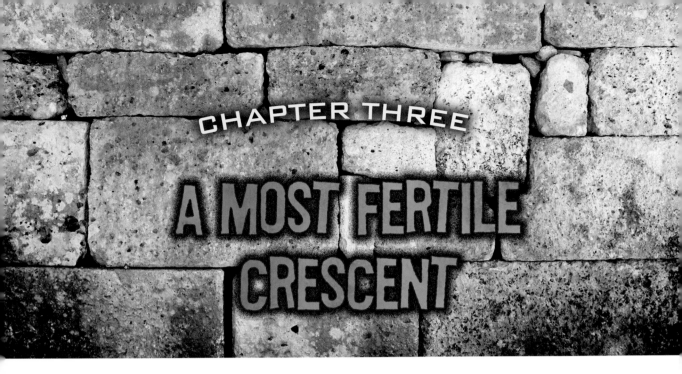

CHAPTER THREE

A MOST FERTILE CRESCENT

Irrigation is the process through which water is taken from one area and channeled into another for the purpose of hydrating soil to encourage the growth of staple crops or other plants. A simple example would be watering your lawn—you are moving water from the pipes inside your house to the ground in your yard in the hope that the grass will grow thicker, greener, and stronger. Farmers must water their crops on a much larger scale, sometimes across hundreds of acres. And humans have been farming—and thus irrigating—for thousands of years.

The Mesopotamians were certainly not the world's first farmers, nor were they the first people to irrigate their land. Some experts believe the earliest communities to build irrigation systems were located in Sumer sometime in the fourth millennium BCE. These systems involved the laborious digging of numerous waterways, some more than a mile long. In the third millennium BCE, the Egyptians built a dam to create a reservoir that would provide water for both irrigation and drinking.

The Mesopotamians made excellent use of their waterways by digging irrigation channels in order to direct water into their farmlands.

Details on clay tablets suggest that the first Mesopotamian irrigation canals were dug in the third millennium BCE. The soil in many Mesopotamian regions was very fertile, especially in the southern areas. This is largely because the Tigris and Euphrates rivers flowed in a southerly direction. When populations and communities close to the rivers became too dense, farmers had to move further outward. They created channels so that the river water would follow them. The well-irrigated land produced excellent crops.

Mesopotamian farmers had to be mindful of one risk of irrigation: the Tigris and Euphrates rivers flooded severely each year when heavy rains fell. Even if the rains occurred in the north, the excess water would accumulate in the south because of the north-to-south current. Another challenging aspect of this annual flooding was that it was nearly impossible to predict when it would occur—flood season lasted roughly from April to June, but not on any specific week, day, or hour. If a farmer's crops received too much water, they would be destroyed. With this in mind, many farmers either built cisterns, which were large holding tanks for extra water, or installed sluice gates, which held the water back in their irrigation channels until the gate doors were lifted. And, like the Egyptians, Mesopotamians built dams.

The basic Mesopotamian irrigation system was a network of channels that began at the Tigris and Euphrates rivers and gradually extended to each individual tract of farmland. Mesopotamian laborers dug thousands of channels over the course of many centuries. Each channel was slightly lower than the one before it, so that gravity would move the water along.

A tool that further helped farmers with their irrigation efforts is known as a shaduf. Developed in the later years of Mesopotamian civilization (after 500 BCE), it was similar in design to a seesaw, except it

Mesopotamian workers dug and maintained thousands of irrigation channels over the centuries, some of which were more than 1 mile (1.6 kilometers) in length.

was much taller, and it had a bucket on one end and a counterweight on the other. It could also pivot left to right. A worker would dip the bucket into a reservoir such as a dam pool or a cistern and then transfer the water over a median area and into an irrigation canal. This may sound like a slow and tedious method, but it was actually a good way of controlling exactly how much water would be used to irrigate a given area. If the counterbalance was of the correct weight, the lifting required very little effort. A fit and able worker could expect to transfer anywhere from 500 to 600 gallons (1,893 to 2,270 liters) of water in one day.

The shaduf enabled farmworkers to transport water by the bucketful from one spot to another with very little effort.

In many areas of the world, people's approach to irrigation has changed little since the time of the Mesopotamians. Farmers still dig canals to channel water from nearby streams and rivers, and the shaduf is still in use in parts of Africa and Asia. In more industrialized nations, mechanized irrigation has taken on many forms. Tough plastic piping is laid underground, and the water is fed into the soil at precise hours determined by electronic timers. Water is also delivered through powerful sprinkler devices that simulate rain showers. Even an ordinary

In the early twentieth century, American archaeologist James Henry Breasted created the nickname "Fertile Crescent" to describe a roughly crescent-shaped area covering not just Mesopotamia but also the Levant—several regions that border the eastern shores of the Mediterranean Sea. The word *fertile* was used in part to denote the high quality of soil that gave rise to a great amount of farming activity. But it also emphasized the rich biodiversity and ideal climate that were found there, especially in ancient times. Toward the end of the last ice age, temperatures rose in many regions and radical changes occurred in the environment. As a result, many of the world's plant and animal species migrated, adapted, or became extinct, and thus many areas became unable to support human life. Tens of thousands of people migrated to the Fertile Crescent region—including Mesopotamia—and slowly began to build the earliest civilizations. This would not have been possible without the rich agricultural potential of the Fertile Crescent.

THE FERTILE CRESCENT

homeowner can build an underground irrigation system to ensure the health of his landscaping—he simply has to program the timer and turn on the water. Everything else happens automatically.

PLOWS

A plow is a device that farmers use to cut, loosen, and otherwise prepare soil for seed growth. Soil that has become too tightly compacted, for example, will not support sturdy crops. Similarly, it is easier to remove weeds, stones, and other undesirable items from soil that has been broken down and turned over. Plowing, therefore, is an essential process of farming.

It is likely that the first plowing tool was a simple stick, perhaps whittled to a point on one end. An ancient farmer would use the stick to poke holes into the earth, drop in seeds, and then fill the holes to cover the seeds. Over time, a few observant individuals probably discovered that seeds grow better in loose soil, and they spent long and arduous hours on their knees as they used the sticks to loosen the soil prior to seeding. Some researchers think the next step in plow evolution was the

A simple plowing tool could be pulled either by a laborer or an animal, loosening the soil and making it easier to seed.

One Mesopotamian laborer (left) *would lead the animals while a second* (middle) *poured seeds into a funnel, and a third* (right) *guided the plow.*

creation of a heavier stick with a two-pronged end (shaped like a Y). One worker would steer the stick by holding the long end while one of the prongs cut through the ground, and another worker would pull the stick along with a rope tied to the other prong.

Mesopotamian farmers may have developed improved plows as far back as the fifth millennium BCE, although there is no proof of this. There is, however, evidence that they used simple plowing devices as far back as the fourth millennium. This was the first effort to formally mechanize farming practices.

The first Mesopotamian plow, which was called an ard, dates to around 3500 BCE. It consisted of three connected heavy sticks, each with a different purpose. The share was somewhat hook shaped, and the point was used to cut through soil. One worker held the staff to guide and steer the ard. Finally, the beam was attached to either a second worker or an animal to pull the device along. The ard was a slight improvement on the earlier plows because each piece was separate and could be replaced as needed. The share often became dull, or the sharpened tip might snap off. Through the three-piece system, a share could be removed and resharpened or replaced altogether. The ard was limited in that it could not penetrate the soil deeply, nor could it truly turn the soil. It merely cut grooves into which seeds could be planted. For this reason, it was also known as a scratch plow.

Seeding took place in the fall or early winter months. In the earliest days of farming, a third worker would follow the ardsmen and drop seeds into the loosened earth by hand. But sometime early in the third millennium, someone came up with the idea of adding a simple seeding device to the plow. It was a vertical funnel attached to the back of the ard. The worker guiding the ard would pour seeds into the funnel, which would distribute the seeds into the freshly cut grooves in a neat line.

As time went on, the Mesopotamians made other improvements to their ard. It is unclear when they began using animals instead of men to pull the plows, but this change likely occurred sometime during the third millennium. There is an ancient image of an ox pulling a plow (the exact time frame is unknown, but possibly the late third millennium), and a man using a seeder funnel as he guides the animal.

Another giant leap in the plow's evolution was the addition of wheels. This not only made the work easier—people could roll the plow instead of dragging it—but also permitted plows to be wider, to have more shares, and thus to cover more land in the same amount of time.

The plow changed little for thousands of years after the Mesopotamians developed it. In the Middle Ages, as humans became more adept at using metals, they replaced wooden parts with iron and steel ones. Metals were tougher, more durable, and sharper for a longer period of time. People also began using curved shares called moldboards, which turned the soil over as it was being plowed. Today's plows are like small vehicles, powered by gas engines and able to prepare hundreds of acres with minimal effort on the part of the driver.

CHAPTER FOUR

BUILDING THE FIRST CIVILIZATIONS

A brick is a basic unit of building material. By piling one brick on top of another and cementing the two together, it is possible to build huge structures that can withstand the most brutal weather conditions and, barring an incident of tremendous devastation, will last for hundreds of years.

Before the creation of bricks, most humans built with wood or piled stone. In Mesopotamia, however, the building material of preference was mud. This was mainly because mud was plentiful, while wood and stone were not.

The earliest Mesopotamians built walls simply by hard-packing mud higher and higher. This method worked just about anywhere and was free of cost, which meant even the poorest citizen could make a home for himself. But building with mud also had serious limitations. A mud structure was unreliable in harsh weather, and it did not stand the test of

Mesopotamians were the first to make extensive use of bricks, erecting structures that stood for thousands of years.

Before brick making became common in Mesopotamia, structures were usually built by hard-packing mud. Unfortunately, dried mud wasn't very stable and required frequent repairs.

time. Also, the groundwater in Mesopotamia had a high salt content, so moisture that came up through the ground had a corrosive effect. The owner of a mud home was often repairing cracks and holes, or even rebuilding entire walls. Also, you could only pile mud so high, and you could only build it so straight. Most mud homes looked crooked and awkward.

Researchers think the Mesopotamians began using bricks as far back as 11,000 years ago. Settlements from this era contain evidence of building blocks of varying size, but most are about 3 inches (7.6 centimeters) thick. Walls built in later years had bricks of a more standardized size. It is important to note that these bricks were not anything like the ones we commonly use today. Early Mesopotamian bricks were also made of mud, sometimes with bits of straw or reed mixed in as a bonding agent, but after they were formed, they were left out in the sun to harden. Again, even the poorest person could make sun-dried bricks and build a fairly durable shelter. Brick structures were sturdier and more handsome than mud homes, but they still broke down after prolonged exposure to the elements.

The real jump in brick-making technology occured in Mesopotamia when someone realized that kiln-fired bricks—those dried within the intense heat of a furnace—had unprecedented strength and longevity. We

A huge step in the evolution of Mesopotamian building came when they discovered the tremendous strength of kiln-fired bricks.

do not know precisely when this important evolutionary step took place, nor is there much evidence as to how people operated their brick-making kilns. But most experts believe that Mesopotamians were using kiln-fired bricks by the middle of the third millennium BCE. By this point, it appears that Mesopotamian builders were using bricks for nearly everything, and brick making was an industry all its own.

Even after the Mesopotamians had more or less mastered the art of brick making, they continued to use mud as a type of cement to hold the

As the Mesopotamians became more confident in their building methods and materials, their design work became bolder and more ornate.

As strange as it may seem, Mesopotamians used mud bricks long after the creation of kiln-fired bricks. The reason was mostly economic—kiln-fired bricks were expensive to make. People had to heat kilns by burning wood, and wood was not common in Mesopotamia. Also, kiln-fired bricks were used only for structures of importance or for those that had to last a long time. For example, people would use kiln-fired bricks to build royal palaces or houses of worship, while mud bricks were used for homes of ordinary people. Mesopotamian builders still followed the mentality that many structures were supposed to be temporary, and it was not unusual to let buildings crumble so that new structures could be built on the same site. There is archaeological evidence of Mesopotamian building sites that were used over and over, to the point where the last structure was erected on little hills of accumulated debris. These little hills are known as tells. They could result not only from structures that had been demolished, but also from those that had collapsed.

bricks together. They would build a wall with mud between each brick and then apply more mud to the face of the wall to give it a smooth and uniform appearance. Sometimes they used clay as a bonding agent, and bitumen—a black and sticky petroleum product similar to tar—was used in monument-type structures. It wasn't until much later that people discovered the strength of mortar.

CHAPTER FIVE

MESOPOTAMIAN MARKINGS, MONEY, MEDICINE, AND MATH

Writing is one of several commonly

used forms of communication. People write in order to take ideas out of their minds and transfer them to someone else's. For example, people write millions of e-mails every day. They also write letters and faxes, books, magazine articles, and so on. There are thousands of written languages around the world, and throughout history there have been many hundreds more. It's hard to imagine life without writing. But where did it all begin?

Some researchers believe humans were trying to communicate through written means more than 30,000 years ago. It is impossible to know for certain, but some archaeological evidence suggests that prehistoric humans may have made marks in stone and wood to denote the passage of time, such as the phases of the moon or the change of seasons. There are also several simple pictures of people and animals

The Mesopotamians were likely the first civilization to attempt the creation of a formal written language.

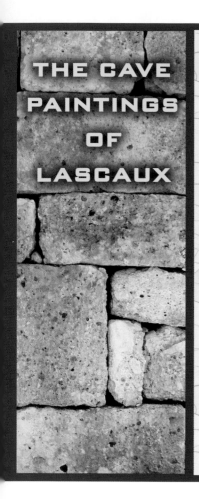

THE CAVE PAINTINGS OF LASCAUX

Long before the Mesopotamians came up with pictographs and cuneiform, humans transferred their thoughts and ideas into simple images. The earliest example we have of such art exists in the famed cave paintings of Lascaux. The Lascaux caves are located in southwestern France, near the tiny village of Montignac. Thought to have been created in the eighteenth millennium BCE, the paintings mostly portray animals but also include humans, geometric shapes, and possibly several renderings of the starry night sky. In September 1940, four young boys and one of their dogs discovered the paintings when they were out playing. Once open to the public, the caves are are now closed to all but scientists since the constant presence of humans began causing the paintings to decay rapidly.

from ancient times, as well as sets of symbols that we still have not deciphered. No one knows why the artists created them, but perhaps the urge to communicate their ideas was powerful enough to drive them to do it.

The Mesopotamians were among the first people to attempt to formalize written language. Clay tablets dating from around 3300 BCE and found in the ancient Mesopotamian city of Uruk show small pictures set in vertical columns. Archaeologists believe these simple pictures were meant to represent ideas. Artists used common images, such as a bird, a sun, or a man's head, as well as more abstract images, such as a circle with a cross inside to represent a sheep. Because this early attempt at writing contained so many pictures, the "language" is referred to as pictograms or pictographs. At the time the clay tablets of Uruk were being used there were already nearly two thousand "characters" in this form of pictography, which suggests that it had been in development for some time. Thus, the Mesopotamians may have been using pictograms long before the archaeological evidence suggests. Stone and clay tokens from as far back as the seventh millennium BCE bear shapes similar to pictographic signs and symbols.

It is difficult to determine the reason why the Mesopotamians were driven to create a written language in the first place. Some experts think people used the symbols as a method of accounting—for example, to keep

The earliest written language in Mesopotamia utilized both readily understandable images and those that were more abstract.

track of agricultural goods or to record exchanges between farmers. At some point, such exchanges may have become too large and detailed to memorize. This type of complex bookkeeping could very well have been the impetus to write things down, and there is early evidence in the form of tablets to support this notion. Keeping people honest may also have been a factor. It is difficult to prove that something did or didn't happen if no written record is available.

Eventually abstract characters became more common than pictograms. Something that is abstract is separate from a known and concrete reality. Many abstractions make no sense until someone teaches us their meaning. Mesopotamian pictography began moving in this direction around the early third millennium BCE. The new system, which was made up of characters whose meaning was not obvious, is known as cuneiform. It is possible the Mesopotamians made this change because drawing birds and feet and other details was just too laborious and time consuming, so it was time to simplify. Whatever the case, cuneiform was the first major step toward written language as we know it today— characters whose meanings need to be taught before they can be understood. By the middle of the third millennium BCE, the Mesopotamians moved cuneiform another step forward by creating characters that represented syllables instead of simple ideas or images. With this latest change, language could be used to communicate all sorts of thoughts and ideas.

The word *cuneiform* comes from the Latin root *cuneus*, which means "wedge." This is because people made the earliest cuneiform characters by pressing the edge of a hard, freshly cut reed into soft clay. Each pressing created a small line that was pointed at one end and slightly wider at the other—wedge shaped. People wrote most cuneiform characters on clay tablets, which they either left in the sun to dry or fired in kilns to harden. Clay tablets were not the only medium for cuneiform writing, however. Mesopotamian writers also scratched characters into both stone and metal. This usually required a tougher tool than a reed—for example, a pointed stick or stone. Whatever material they used, their instrument was called a stylus.

Cuneiform was the standard language of the Mesopotamians for thousands of years. The Sumerians, Assyrians, and Babylonians also used and developed the language, and eventually it spread through the Middle

The Mesopotamian language eventually evolved into a style known as cuneiform. The word comes from the Latin cuneus, *meaning "wedge," and refers to the edge of a cut reed that was used to press the characters into soft clay.*

East to Persia. People wrote letters on small clay tablets, which they then—believe it or not—slipped into larger clay envelopes. In fact, the world's oldest known epic poems were written in cuneiform on clay tablets.

Cuneiform expanded further when people in different parts of Mesopotamia developed variations. Each region would add to the collective language in its own way, often without the knowledge of neighboring regions. The upside of this practice was that it provided proof of cuneiform's success. Eventually, a more formal alphabet may have been developed in the area of modern-day Syria and Palestine around 1600. Whether or not it had roots in cuneiform is unclear, but it certainly provided the seeds for other alphabets around the world.

MONEY

Money is at the very heart of the modern world. It is the medium by which we buy and sell nearly all goods—food, clothes, gasoline, property, and more. Money can also buy a variety of services, such as having a house cleaned, a car washed, or a lawn cut. It is hard to imagine life without it.

It is generally agreed that the Mesopotamians were the first people to come up with a formal monetary system. (Scholars disagree on the location of the earliest physical coinage. Possibilities include Anatolia, western Turkey, and Egypt). It is impossible to know exactly what inspired the idea in Mesopotamia. It might have become too difficult for people to agree on the relative value of certain items during trades. For example, if a Mesopotamian farmer with a spare sack of barley wanted some fruit from another farmer, how would they decide what a fair trade would be? How many oranges would be equal to the sack of barley? Perhaps people decided to place an object "in between" such transactions—an object against which all other items could be valued.

In ancient times—just like today—most people desired precious metals. Because of this, these materials were considered valuable. The most common money metals were gold, silver, lead, and bronze. To a lesser degree, people used copper and tin. Through the exchange of these metals, a Mesopotamian citizen could hire laborers, buy land, or pay his taxes. By the second millennium BCE, silver rather than gold had become the most common metal for the purpose of exchange and purchase. Other metals were still used, but silver was the most plentiful.

In this ancient stone carving, Assyrians are seen weighing precious metals, which were used as money. The more you had in terms of weight, the more you could buy with it.

The value of a precious metal was based on its weight—the more it weighed, the greater its buying power. Mesopotamians did not weigh objects by the standard system (pounds, ounces) or the metric system (grams, kilograms) that we use today. Instead, they had a basic unit, known as a shekel (from the ancient Babylonian term *shiqlu*), which may have first been used around 3000 BCE. Experts believe the shekel represented just under 0.3 percent of a modern ounce. How the Mesopotamians determined exact

SHEKELS REVISITED

The word *shekel* is not only a name for a basic unit of weight in Mesopotamia. It also refers to certain coinage, both ancient and modern. Although the Mesopotamians were the first to use the term, ancient Hebrews also used it to designate a certain weight (which varied from area to area). Around the biblical time of Jesus, they also began using it as a name for one of their most common silver coins. Soon the word took on a broader and more generic usage, as evidenced by the fact that other ancient cultures, including the Edomites and the Phoenicians, made use of it both as a unit of weight and as currency. Today, the shekel—also spelled *sheqel*—is the official currency in Israel. This began in 1980 and then changed again in 1985, when the new denomination was named the "Israel new shekel." The Israel shekel also exists in paper form, currently in four denominations.

Coins were not used in Mesopotamia until the first millennium BCE. This one, from Babylon some time around 325 BCE, depicts Alexander the Great holding a bow and scepter.

weights is unknown, since there are no remaining scales from the period. However, archaeologists have found some counterweights, which might have been used for rough comparison—not a very precise method at all! Scientists believe that the silver traded in Mesopotamian times was only about 95 to 98 percent pure (as opposed to fine silver today, which is nearly 100 percent pure), probably because ancient metallurgists did not have the technology to remove all impurities.

One of the most common types of Mesopotamian currency was simple bracelets or rings. A citizen might, for example, carry a metal ring of lesser metal (say, copper or tin), and on it would be a collection of smaller bracelets made of silver. The average weight of a money ring was between one and twenty shekels (although over fifty was not unknown), though five to ten shekels was the most common weight. Sometimes silver was cast as a spiral coil, which people could break up as needed.

A rarer form of currency was the ingot—basically a rectangular block of metal. Government agents determined the weight of each ingot. Large ingots were probably not often used in everyday transactions, as they would have been far too heavy—the average Mesopotamian businessman would quickly develop a bad back if he had to carry a few around all day!

By the middle of the first millennium BCE, Mesopotamians were using actual coins, as were the people of other cultures, including the Greeks, Romans, and Chinese. People made molds from clay and filled them with molten metals such as copper, gold, silver, and electrum (a pale yellowish alloy made from gold and silver). They also produced coins by striking heated metals with a hammer. In colonial America, starting in the seventeenth century, people used presses for coin making. The press method is still used today, albeit in a highly technological form that involves tremendous amounts of pressure and very accurate striking. Gold and silver are no longer the metals of choice, as they have become more valuable in weight than the coins' face values. Instead, most modern coins are made from zinc, nickel, copper, or some combination of those metals.

MEDICINE

Since the time of the earliest humans, there has been illness. And for most of history, the human body has remained shrouded in mystery. Even today, there are many aspects of illness that we neither understand nor treat successfully. Take viruses, for example. A virus is a tiny infectious agent that essentially hijacks the cells of its host for the purpose of making as many copies of itself as possible. Viruses have probably existed since the dawn of time, yet we still do not know what makes them tick or, more importantly, how we can eradicate them. Nevertheless, you have a better chance of recovering from an illness today than ever before, and modern medical knowledge is based on the combined experience of physicians throughout history.

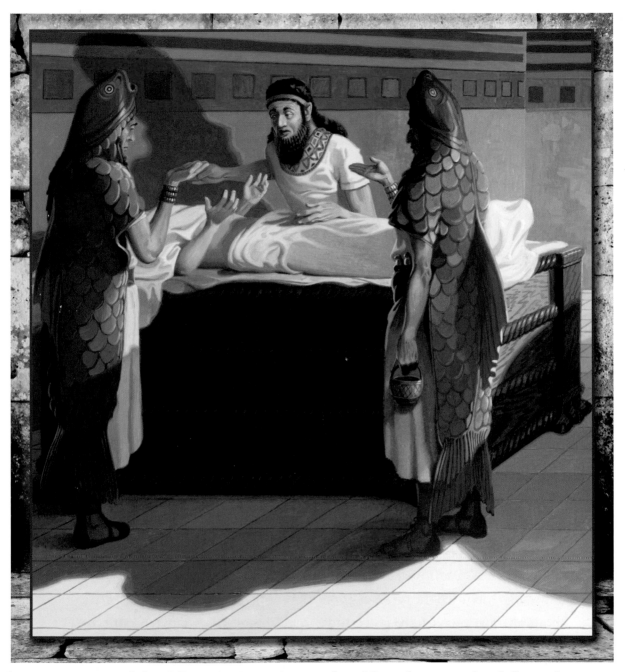

Mesopotamians believed illness to be the act of angry gods, and those who were struck with illness to be deserving due to their sinful actions.

The Mesopotamians were the first people to attempt formalization of medical treatment. Since their knowledge of the human body was very limited, they based their approaches on ideas that may seem misguided today but were central to Mesopotamian culture at the time. For example, if a person became ill, it was generally believed he was a victim of either some form of dark magic or the anger of the gods. People theorized that his illness was justified because he lived his life in a sinful, shameful manner.

The Mesopotamians' general approach to medical treatment consisted of two basic parts—the practical and the magical. To facilitate this, two types of "doctors" were required—an *asu* and an *ashipu*. The asu bore a closer resemblance to today's physicians in the sense that he was responsible for applying medications. The ashipu's job, on the other hand, was a bit more abstract—he would examine the patient's symptoms and then make predictions about the seriousness of the condition and whether or not the patient would live. The ashipu would base his bold and miraculous "insights" on outside factors such as the weather, the time of day, or the day of the year.

As unbelievable as it may seem, the ashipu was considered the leader in medical treatment—and was more respected in Mesopotamian society overall—while the asu was regarded as somewhat secondary. The ashipu would ultimately dictate treatment, and the asu was expected to follow those orders. Ashipu treatments involved practical medications, but they also included the tying of knots, the conjuring of benevolent spirits, communication with the gods, and ceremonies designed to drive out the forces of evil. Numerology—the study of numbers and their possible influence on various events—also likely played a role here, figuring into matters such as how many drops of a certain medication should be used or what day of the month was the best time for rendering treatment. The Mesopotamians considered the ashipu to be a man of science. In time, the asu as an individual probably ceased to exist, and the ashipu absorbed his duties.

THE POOR MAN AND THE MAYOR

There is a somewhat humorous Mesopotamian story that was probably first told around the middle of the first millennium BCE. It's about a poor man who seeks revenge against a greedy mayor through "medical means." It seems the poor man becomes aware of a wound the mayor received and goes to the mayor's home disguised as an ashipu. His disguise and mannerisms are apparently convincing, for the mayor's guards let the man pass without further question. The imposter then examines the wounds and makes a cursory diagnosis. This, too, impresses all present, and the "doctor" is left alone with the mayor. He then makes the claim that he can render an effective treatment, but that it will only work in darkness, and only if the mayor is bound. In darkness, the poor citizen proceeds to tie the sadistic mayor's hands and feet and beat him mercilessly. In spite of the mayor's cries of pain, his guards do not come to his rescue. Once satisfied, the poor man flees the premises. One can only assume he is in good spirits thereafter.

Medications consisted of common materials found in the region, including herbs and other plant matter, animal parts, and a few minerals. Every part of a plant was utilized—roots, stems, leaves, seeds, fruits, and so on—and might be ground into fine powder, boiled, dried out, or used fresh. Commonly used animal parts included fat, blood, bones, milk, fur, and tallow, also rendered in various forms. Minerals such as salt and saltpeter would be ground up or boiled. Herbs, however, were the most commonly used form of medicine, probably because they were widespread, easy to obtain, and diverse.

Mesopotamians applied medications in any number of ways. Oral application—swallowing—was common. A more uncomfortable type of application was a suppository or enema—the medication was inserted at the *other* end of the body (an unpleasant proposition in the age before painkillers). With the oral method, at least, the ashipu or asu might mix the medicine with something more palatable, such as beer, wine, or honey. Even swallowing a mouthful of vinegar was more preferable than using a suppository. For topical ailments, such as minor cuts and scrapes, the Mesopotamians developed a variety of herbal lotions, creams, and salves. And it should be noted that while all of these remedies may seem like quaint folk medicine, some of them not only had the desired effect, but also lasted, in one form or another, to this day.

There is little evidence that Mesopotamian physicians used advanced medical instruments or performed surgery. This is logical, given the fact that they considered most ailments to be the will of greater beings—thus, if the gods wished you to recover, then you'd recover. And while it is likely that the majority of treatments had little positive effect (and patients eventually recovered on their own), the Mesopotamians left behind an incredible contribution: detailed lists of both medicines and symptoms

Early surgical tools were often made of bronze and crudely forged, likely making their use very painful for their patients. Fortunately, all historical evidence suggests most Mesopotamian healers rarely performed surgery.

that helped future health professionals in their quest to determine the best strategies to combat human illness.

MATHEMATICS

It is very likely that humans have always used mathematics. Even in the earliest times, counting was a basic mathematical function that helped people get through each day. For example, counting the nights until the next full moon, or keeping track of how long food stores would last until it became necessary to hunt or harvest again, were crucial to human survival.

The Mesopotamians are believed to be the first of the ancient cultures to take mathematics beyond this basic point and to utilize math's inherent power to create complex systems and to accomplish greater objectives. Even before they developed writing, Mesopotamian businessmen would use small lumps of dried clay, known as tokens, to keep track of important figures during agricultural transactions. Soon they were using math in everyday administrative functions, including aspects of metrology—the science of measuring. Some evidence suggests that the Mesopotamians were crazy about measuring stuff, including weights, distances, and volumes. By the end of the third millennium BCE, the people of Sumer were routinely writing down mathematical functions in cuneiform.

Mesopotamian mathematicians used two very different mathematical systems. One was known as the sexagesimal, or base-60, system. In this system, all functions were based on the number 60. The number of minutes in an hour (60), for example, or the number of degrees in a circle (360, or 60 x 6), came from this. They also used the decimal, or base-10, system—with all functions based on the number 10—that we are familiar with today.

Archaeological evidence shows that the Mesopotamians designed reference tables extensively. Tablets from as far back as the mid-second millennium chart figures for multiplication, divisions, square roots, cube roots, ratios, reciprocals, and other operations. Also very common were problem texts—mathematical problems woven into written language. Often the solution would be given at the end and explained

This tablet illustrates a number of geometric problems—specifically to determine an area—being worked out. Since there is also a text element to each problem, it is possible this tablet was used by a student learning basic mathematics.

in step-by-step fashion—followed by another problem *without* a solution. It is likely that these tablets belonged to Mesopotamian students who were expected to study the first problem and then to solve the others on their own. The students' calculations can still be seen in the margins of some tablets—an early example of scratch paper!

One revolutionary way in which the Mesopotamians formalized written mathematics was through the use of the place values. This meant each digit to the left of the last number had a higher decimal value within the base-10 system. For example, the 5 in the number 7,253 was considered to have a value of five tens (thus, 50). The 2, then, had a value of two hundreds (200), and so on. This is common, basic math for us today, but until the Mesopotamians began using it in the late third millennium BCE, it did not exist. They were likely also the first civilization to regularly use fractions—the dividing of wholes—which became essential to their measuring efforts. The Mesopotamians also got plenty of use out of *pi*, although they gave it an erroneous value— first 3, then the much closer 3 ⅛.

OUR HERO ZERO

Incredible as it may seem, Mesopotamian mathematicians were the first to recognize the need for a symbol to represent the value of zero. Originally, they only left an empty space, but that led to some confusion. How much space was enough? How little was too little? After a time they began using simple symbols, but even these were not adequate. It would not be until much later that the people of either India or Indochina created a set of numeric characters that included formal 0, and the earliest examples of the 0 symbol in cuneiform come from the seventh century BCE. Nevertheless, the Mesopotamians at least acknowledged the importance of the zero sum.

By the first millennium BCE, Mesopotamian mathematicians had begun to realize that they could use advanced functions beyond the concrete and into the theoretical. People could use theoretical math to explore ideas in astronomy, physics, and other branches of science. Even if they did not unearth all the answers they sought, the fact that they ventured into previously unknown territory is a testament to their intelligence and ambition. Virtually all our day-to-day math is still built on the foundation of the decimal system that the Mesopotamians devised.

circa 8000 BCE—The first communities settle along the base of the Zagros Mountains, thus marking the beginning of the Mesopotamian region.

ca. 6500 BCE—The earliest evidence of written language, in the form of stone and clay tokens with signs and symbols similar to later pictographs, is created.

ca. 5000 BCE—The first wheel, which started as a potter's wheel, is developed.

ca. 4000–3500 BCE—Boats are most likely being used in Mesopotamia, as evidenced by a small model found by archaeologists.

ca. 3500 BCE—Pictographs evolve from simple, direct images to more abstract symbols.

ca. 3500 BCE—Mesopotamians are using kiln-fired bricks.

ca. 3400 BCE—Mesopotamians are using ards in farming.

ca. 3200 BCE—Wheels are first used on a vehicle.

ca. 3100 BCE—Animals are being used to pull whceled vehicles.

ca. 3000 BCE—Mesopotamians are probably using a unit of weight known as the shekel.

ca. 3000 BCE—Sumerians are routinely writing mathematical functions.

ca. 2750 BCE—Mesopotamians begin digging irrigation canals.

ca. 2500 BCE—Mesopotamians are using precious metals as currency.

ca. 2250 BCE—Seeder funnels are added to plows.

ca. 2250 BCE—Silver is the most common metal used for currency.

ca. 2000 BCE—People begin using the place-value system in mathematics.

ca. 600 BCE—Mesopotamians, as well as other cultures, begin routinely using coins.

539 BCE—Mesopotamia falls under the control of the Persian Empire.

GLOSSARY

ard—An early plow featuring three connected heavy sticks of differing shapes and purposes. See *beam*, *share*, and *staff*.

ashipu—The Mesopotamian equivalent of a medicine man, who used not only practical symptomology but also various sources of magic—including numerology and astrology—to determine treatments for the ill.

asu—The Mesopotamian equivalent of a modern physician, mostly responsible for applying remedies to the ill.

beam—Part of an ard tied to an animal or worker so the ard could be pulled forward.

cisterns—Sealed holding tanks for water or other liquids.

coracle (quffa)—A small boat with a shallow, bowl-like body, a mast set near the center, and holes through which ropes and sails would be tied.

cuneiform—A Mesopotamian system of writing that utilized short lines pressed into soft clay by way of a cut reed and featured characters whose meanings were purely abstract.

decimal (base-10) system—A mathematical system based on the number 10.

keleks—Mesopotamian boats built for sea and ocean use. They featured strong woods caulked so as to be watertight, plus inflated animal skins tied to the bottom and sides for added buoyancy.

kiln—A furnace used to dry clay tablets, bricks, and similar items.

pictograms—Simple images that form a type of early language.

scratch plow—The colloquial name for an ard.

sexagesimal (base-60) system—A mathematical system based on the number 60.

shaduf—A tall, seesaw-like device with a large bucket on one end and a counterweight on the other, used to scoop and transfer water from natural reservoirs or cisterns into irrigation channels.

share—The hook-shaped part of an ard, used to cut and loosen soil.

shekel—In Mesopotamian times, a basic unit of weight. Today's equivalent would be roughly two-fifths of an ounce.

sluice gates—Small gateways set into water channels, with a door that can be lifted to permit or restrict flow as needed.

staff—The handle part of an ard, used to steer and guide it.

stylus—Any item used by the Mesopotamians to create written characters, usually on clay, stone, wood, or metal.

tells—Small hills that have accumulated as a result of material from demolished or collapsed structures.

BOOKS

Hunter, Dr. Erica C. D. *Ancient Mesopotamia* (Cultural Atlas for Young People). New York: Chelsea House Publishers, 2007.

Kerrigan, Michael. *Mesopotamians* (Ancients in Their Own Words). New York: Marshall Cavendish, 2010.

Nardo, Don. *Peoples and Empires of Ancient Mesopotamia* (Lucent Library of Historical Eras). Farmington Hills, MI: Lucent Books, 2009.

Steele, Philip, and John Farndon. *Mesopotamia* (DK Eyewitness Books). New York: DK Publishing, 2007.

WEBSITES

www.historyforkids.org/learn/westasia/history/earlydynastic.htm

The Mesopotamians page on the History for Kids website. Gives good general information on the early dynastic period, links for other subjects, and further reading recommendations.

---

http://mesopotamia.mrdonn.org/

Content-rich site concerning all aspects of Mesopotamia, including geography, history, daily life, lesson plans, and much more.

---

www.kidskonnect.com/content/view/257/27/

Kids Connect site on Mesopotamia, with dozens of links covering all aspects of ancient Mesopotamia life and history.

INDEX

About the Author

Wil Mara is an award-winning author who has written many educational titles for young readers, covering subjects such as history, geography, animals, social issues, and biographies of notable people. More information about his work can be found at www.wilmara.com.